RACE TO MOUNT EVEREST

BY JANIE HAVEMEYER

MOMENTUM

Published by The Child's World®
1980 Lookout Drive • Mankato, MN 56003-1705
800-599-READ • www.childsworld.com

Photographs ©: AP Images, cover, 1, 17, 20,
28; Shutterstock Images, 5, 12, 18, 25; PA Wire
URN:23887423/Press Association/AP Images, 6;
Red Line Editorial, 8; Royal Geographical Society/
Contributor/Royal Geographical Society (with IBG)/
Getty Images, 9; PA/AP Images, 10; Pasang Geljen
Sherpa/AP Images, 14; iStockphoto, 22; ullstein
bild Dti./ullstein bild/Getty Images, 26

ISBN 9781503832237
LCCN 2018962834

Printed in the United States of America
PA02421

ABOUT THE AUTHOR

Janie Havemeyer is an author of many books for young readers. Janie has a
master's degree in education and has taught in schools and museums. Janie
lives in San Francisco, California, and is married to a mountain climber.

CONTENTS

MOMENTUM

FAST FACTS

Where Is Mount Everest?

► Mount Everest is in the Himalayan mountain range in Asia. The mountain range is between Nepal and Tibet.

What's It Like on Mount Everest?

► Mount Everest is 29,035 feet (8,850 m) high.

► Winds on Mount Everest have been recorded at 200 miles per hour (321 kmh).

► Temperatures on Mount Everest range from –31 degrees Fahrenheit (–35°C) to –4 degrees Fahrenheit (–20°C).

Climbers and Mount Everest

► Climbers start to use bottled oxygen at 23,000 feet (7,010 m) because the air has less oxygen at this **altitude**.

► Most of the deaths on Mount Everest occur in what people call the "death zone."[1] This is an area near the top of the mountain. There are many dangers in this area. One danger is a lack of oxygen.

► **Avalanches** are the most common cause of death on Mount Everest, followed by falling.

**Hundreds of people try to climb ►
Mount Everest each year.**

CHAPTER ONE

THE DEATH ZONE

Thirty-three-year-old Edmund Hillary peered up at the top of Mount Everest, the tallest mountain in the world. The rough wind tore at the snow surrounding him. It sent the white flakes drifting across the mountain's surface. It was May 29, 1953.

Hillary and his climbing partner Tenzing Norgay were far above the clouds at 28,700 feet (8,750 m). There was no time to waste. Climbers called this area of Mount Everest the "death zone." If they stayed too long at this altitude, they could die from lack of oxygen. The oxygen bottles strapped to their backs would help them survive—until the bottles were empty.

Hillary and Tenzing were part of a British climbing **expedition** to be the first people to reach Mount Everest's **summit**. A tight rope stretched between them. If one of them fell or slipped, the other could stop him. They took turns being in front.

◄ **Edmund Hillary was from New Zealand. He started mountain climbing when he was in high school.**

Before them lay deep snow. A thin crust covered the snow's surface. When the fragile crust gave way, they sank in up to their waists. It took a lot of strength to step forward. Hillary remembered what expedition leader John Hunt had said: put safety above everything. But climbing Mount Everest had been Hillary's lifelong dream, and he wanted to reach the summit. "This is Everest and you've got to take a few risks!" he thought.[2]

COMMON CAUSES OF DEATH ON MOUNT EVEREST

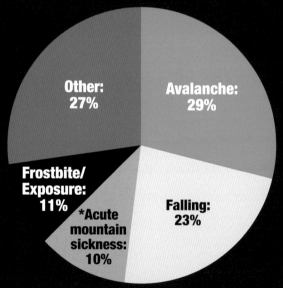

Other: 27%

Avalanche: 29%

Frostbite/ Exposure: 11%

*Acute mountain sickness: 10%

Falling: 23%

*Acute mountain sickness can happen to climbers when they are in a high altitude. Severe acute mountain sickness can affect a person's brain and lungs.

▲ **Hillary and Tenzing had to work together to climb the mountain.**

Then Hillary heard a loud cracking sound. The block of icy snow he was standing on broke off from the slope, pulling him backward. Hillary's heart started pounding. He prayed he and Tenzing would not be Mount Everest's next victims, buried on the mountain so close to reaching their goal.

CHAPTER TWO

FIRST TO THE TOP

Months before the expedition, in March, Hillary nervously stepped onto the green lawns of the British Embassy in Kathmandu, the capital of Nepal. He was about to meet John Hunt, the expedition leader, for the first time. Hunt shook his hand. He was warm and friendly. Hillary greeted the other climbers and introduced himself to Tenzing. Tenzing had a reputation as a skilled Sherpa climber. The Sherpas had been living at the base of Mount Everest for more than 500 years. Tenzing had helped with other people's attempts to climb to the top of Mount Everest. Hillary was happy Tenzing would be helping them, too.

British mountaineers had been trying to summit Mount Everest since the 1920s. In the 1950s, climbers from other countries, such as Switzerland, began to try. This interest sparked a competition to see which nation could summit the tall mountain first.

◄ **Years after the climb up Mount Everest, Tenzing (right) came to England. John Hunt greeted him.**

▲ **Climbers rest at different camps as they journey up Mount Everest.**

Nepal only allowed one group to go each year. In 1953, the British were trying again. Hillary looked around at the equipment and supplies. The team looked prepared for the adventure, and Hillary felt a knot of excitement grow in his stomach.

The British expedition traveled miles from Kathmandu to the base of Mount Everest. Climbers and **porters** moved up winding, rocky paths, crossing rivers and valleys. For the next 17 days, the men ate meals together and practiced working as a team. On March 29, Hillary poked his head out of his tent. Finally, in the morning sunlight, he could see Mount Everest up close. He studied the Lhotse Face below the summit. It was a steep slope of snow and ice. Below that he saw the Khumbu **Icefall**, one of the most dangerous places on the mountain. It was filled with blocks of ice called **seracs** and seemingly bottomless **crevasses** where a person could disappear. His heart pounded with excitement and fear.

SHERPAS

The Sherpa people have lived at the base of the Himalayan mountains for centuries. Many of them are good climbers. They grow up in villages at high altitudes. Their lungs have adapted to need less oxygen than people who live in lower altitudes. One-third of the deaths on Mount Everest have been Sherpas.

CHAPTER THREE

A PARTNERSHIP

Hunt picked Hillary to lead a small group to find a safe route up the Khumbu Icefall. By mid-April, they were hard at work, cutting steps into the creaking ice with their axes. This would make it easier for Sherpas to climb up with supplies for the camps. They placed pine logs and aluminum ladders across crevasses. One day Hillary heard a crack. A serac split in half and crashed to the ground just 50 feet (15.2 m) from where his group stood. Blocks of ice rushed past them and just missed killing them.

Hillary liked teaming up with Tenzing whenever he could. He saw that Tenzing was quick on his feet and had the same drive to succeed as Hillary. Tenzing got Hillary's trust when Hillary jumped over a narrow crevasse. A large block of ice sheared off.

◄ In 2013, Sherpa climbers went up the Khumbu Icefall.

It sent him flying downward. Tenzing pulled the rope tight and saved his life.

By late April, the expedition had set up four camps on the mountain. The first one was called Base Camp, and it was at the bottom of the icefall. On the morning of May 7, Hunt called everyone together at Base Camp. He had important news. May 15 would be the date for the summit attempt. First, the expedition would move to Camp Four, which was located 21,200 feet (6,460 m) up the mountain. From there, climbers would break into small teams to prepare a route to 26,000 feet (7,920 m)—about 3,000 feet (910 m) below the summit. Finally, Hunt announced what they had all be waiting to hear. Two climbers would try for the summit: Charles Evans and Tom Bourdillon. Evans was an experienced climber and doctor. Bourdillon was an expert in using the oxygen equipment. Hunt had confidence in them. But he told Hillary and Tenzing that they would have a chance to climb to the summit later if Evans and Bourdillon failed. However, there was still work to do before anyone could start the journey farther upward.

Hillary (left) and Hunt spent a lot of time thinking ▶ about how best to climb Mount Everest.

CHAPTER FOUR

THE RACE IS ON

Hunt focused his binoculars on a spot below Mount Everest's peak. It was a clear day. Hunt could just make out the ridge where he wanted to set up a camp for the final climb. But first he needed a climber to figure out how to get there. He picked George Lowe to lead the charge. Lowe would carve a path up the Lhotse Face. He would also set up more camps along the way. There wasn't a moment to waste. The summit target day was five days away.

But as soon as Lowe and his team left on May 10, the weather turned. Snow poured down from the sky. Hunt watched the group's progress with his powerful binoculars. He saw how the group struggled through waist-high snowdrifts. When they cut steps in the ice, the steps disappeared under layers of fresh snow. Breathing at this altitude was very hard, even with oxygen tanks.

◀ **People have to rely on their group members'
help when climbing Mount Everest.**

▲ **Before starting the journey up Mount Everest, the British expedition team climbed other nearby mountains.**

But finally, on May 11, Lowe reached 22,000 feet (6,700 m), where he set up Camp Five. It took him five and a half hours to climb another 600 feet (183 m) and set up Camp Six. Afterward, Lowe was so exhausted he slept for 15 hours.

The next day it snowed again. Other expeditions had been defeated by weather. If the climbers didn't make an attempt to reach the summit soon, they might have to give up. The **monsoon** season would come to Mount Everest in late May, bringing heavy snow and high winds. But on May 13, the sky was clear.

Lowe picked up speed and made it to 24,000 feet (7,300 m) by May 14 and set up Camp Seven. That night, he radioed Hunt promising more progress. But the next day Lowe had trouble moving. His body felt like lead. It appeared that his brain could have been affected by his long stay at high altitudes. Another British climber, Wilfrid Noyce, was sent up to help. He gave Lowe sardines to boost his energy, but Lowe was so tired that he fell into a deep sleep before he could eat the food. Noyce couldn't wake him, so he rushed down to report back to Hunt. May 15 came and went, and Evans and Bourdillon hadn't started their climb to the summit. The expedition looked like it might be tipping toward defeat.

CLIMBING AND FOOD

At high altitudes, climbers lose their appetite. It is a struggle to eat to stay fit. But having enough food while climbing is important. In 1953, a new technique was used to pack food. It was called vacuum packing. This made food packets light because all the air was sucked out of a package before sealing. A common daily serving of vacuum-packed food for two men weighed 4 pounds (1.8 kg).

CHAPTER FIVE

FALSE HOPE

Noyce took over for Lowe. In five days, Noyce had made a route up to 26,000 feet (7,920 m). Tents were set up on a windswept plateau that became Camp Eight. On the night of May 21, members of the expedition huddled inside their tents. Strong winds shrieked and roared outside. For the next few days, everyone was busy preparing for the first climb to the summit.

As the first rays of sun hit the plateau on May 26, Evans and Bourdillon put on their boots, gloves, and **crampons**. But when Evans drew a breath from his oxygen tank, he choked. It took Bourdillon more than one hour to fix the problem, which was a damaged oxygen supply valve. They set out late, but still made good time climbing upward, weaving around the rocks and boulders. But as the slope became steeper, they slowed.

◀ **Sherpas are hired to help climbers with things such as setting up camps.**

Lowe was watching their progress from Camp Eight. When he saw two tiny figures climbing steadily up and over the South Summit, he shouted, "Tom and Charles have made it!"[3] Everyone at Camp Eight began to rejoice. Then the clouds rolled in, hiding the two climbers from view.

But Evans and Bourdillon still had more than 300 feet (90 m) to climb, although they had already set a world altitude record on the South Summit. It was 1:20 p.m. Evans estimated that it would take three more hours to get to the summit. They only had two and a half hours of oxygen left. Evans knew they couldn't climb without oxygen in their tanks, but Bourdillon thought they could. They had come this far, and Bourdillon believed that they had to try. The two men debated. It was hard to think clearly at that altitude. Bourdillon considered setting out by himself without Evans, but Evans convinced him not to. The pair headed back to camp. Now, Hillary and Tenzing would have their chance to climb to the summit.

THE PHYSICAL DIFFICULTIES OF CLIMBING MOUNT EVEREST

At high altitudes there's a decreased amount of oxygen. Not getting enough oxygen can cause confusion, headaches, and reduced brain function.

The heart has to work harder and faster to pump blood because of the high altitude.

A climber's breathing can be five or six times faster than normal when he or she reaches the top of Mount Everest.

High altitudes can lead to a loss of appetite and nausea.

The cold temperatures on Mount Everest can cause frostbite and hypothermia.

CHAPTER SIX

THE HIGHEST POINT ON EARTH

Three days later, on May 29, Hillary and Tenzing sat at the same altitude on the South Summit. It was 9:00 a.m. Before them stretched the final crest of Mount Everest. It took them one hour and 20 minutes to reach the last obstacle: a 40-foot (12 m) rock wall below the summit. Hillary checked his oxygen cylinders. They had three hours left. He studied the rock face. They needed to climb it quickly.

A huge icy **cornice** on the edge of the rock had started to split away from the rock, forming a narrow gap between the rock and ice. If he leaned back against the cornice and used his hands and feet to wiggle his way up, he could reach the top. But if the cornice broke loose, he would tumble down the mountain. He looked at Tenzing, who nodded. Hillary began to climb— digging his crampons into rock, then lifting his body upward.

◄ **Hillary and Tenzing checked their supplies before starting the climb to Mount Everest's summit.**

▲ **Hillary and Tenzing were honored for their accomplishment.**

When he reached the top of the wall, he helped Tenzing up. The two climbers stopped to catch their breath. They still were not at the summit.

They plodded on until, finally, at 11:30 a.m., the slope flattened out. They could see the country of Tibet on one side and the valleys of Nepal on the other. On their right was a 40-foot (12 m) bump—the top of Mount Everest. They took weary steps toward it. The bump was just big enough for them to both stand on. They hugged each other. They had made it to the highest point on Earth: 29,035 feet (8,850 m). They enjoyed the moment and the view stretching before them for 15 minutes before heading down.

News of their success traveled fast. British officials heard the news on June 2, which was also the day Queen Elizabeth II was crowned. Newspapers around the world spread the news. Mount Everest had been conquered. Britain rejoiced. Hillary became a national hero and was knighted by the queen. Both India and Nepal claimed Tenzing as their climbing hero, since he'd lived in both countries. The two climbers became the public faces of one of Britain's proudest accomplishments. As the *New York Times* reported, it was "the conquest of the last unconquered spot on earth."[4] The success of the expedition made more people want to climb Mount Everest. As of 2018, thousands of climbers had made it to the top.

THINK ABOUT IT

► Do you think it would be possible to climb Mount Everest without the help of a team? Explain your answer.

► How might have Evans and Bourdillon's unsuccessful summit climb have helped Hillary and Tenzing reach the top?

► Was it fair that Hillary and Tenzing got most of the credit for being the first to summit Mount Everest? Explain your answer.

GLOSSARY

altitude (AL-ti-tood): Altitude is the height of anything above sea level or ground on Earth. Being at a high altitude can harm people's health.

avalanches (AV-uh-lanch-ez): Avalanches are large masses of snow and ice that tumble down a mountain. Some climbers die from avalanches.

cornice (KOR-nis): A cornice is a ledge of snow on the edge of a mountain ridge. Hillary and Tenzing encountered a cornice.

crampons (KRAM-ponz): Crampons are spiked iron plates worn on boots to keep climbers from slipping. The crampons helped the climber step firmly onto the ice.

crevasses (kruh-VASZ-es): Crevasses are breaks or deep cracks in the ice. Climbers have to watch out for crevasses.

expedition (ek-spuh-DISH-uhn): An expedition is a long trip made for a specific reason. The climbers were on an expedition to Mount Everest.

icefall (EYESS-fawl): An icefall is a very steep part of a glacier or icy slope with deep cracks. The Khumbu Icefall is a dangerous place on Mount Everest.

monsoon (mahn-SOON): A monsoon is a seasonal heavy rainfall and wind in places such as southern Asia. The monsoon season on Mount Everest brings a lot of snow.

porters (POR-turs): Porters are people hired to carry things. Porters carried the supplies up Mount Everest.

seracs (si-RAKS): Seracs are blocks of ice along glacier crevasses. The Khumbu Icefall has seracs.

summit (SUHM-it): A summit is the top or the highest point. Climbers reached the summit of the mountain.

SOURCE NOTES

1. "Why Climbers Die on Mount Everest." *Science Daily.* ScienceDaily, 15 Dec. 2008. Web. 6 Nov. 2018.

2. Edmund Hillary. *High Adventure.* London: Hodder & Stoughton, 1995. Print. 214–219.

3. Mick Conefrey. *Everest 1953: The Epic Story of the First Ascent.* Seattle, WA: Mountaineers Books, 2013. Print. 183.

4. "An End and A Beginning." *New York Times.* New York Times Company, 3 June 1953. Web. 28 Sept. 2018.

TO LEARN MORE

BOOKS

Francis, Angela Sangma. *Everest.* London: Flying Eye Books, 2018.

Medina, Nico. *Where Is Mount Everest?*
New York, NY: Grosset & Dunlap, 2015.

Rajczak Nelson, Kristen. *Climbing Mount Everest.*
New York, NY: Gareth Stevens Publishing, 2014.

WEBSITES

Visit our website for links about Mount Everest: **childsworld.com/links**

*Note to Parents, Teachers, and Librarians: We routinely verify our Web links to make sure
they are safe and active sites. So encourage your readers to check them out!*

INDEX